SCIENTIFIC AMERICAN | EDUCATIONAL PUBLISHING

SCIENTIFIC AMERICAN INVESTIGATES CAREERS IN SCIENCE

ARCHAEOLOGIST

BY ROSIE BANKS

Published in 2025 by The Rosen Publishing Group
in association with Scientific American Educational Publishing
2544 Clinton Street, Buffalo NY 14224

Library of Congress Cataloging-in-Publication Data
Names: Banks, Rosie, 1978- author.
Title: Archaeologist / Rosie Banks.
Description: New York : Scientific American Educational Publishing, an imprint of Rosen Publishing, [2025] | Series: Scientific american investigates careers in science | Includes index.
Identifiers: LCCN 2024030553 (print) | LCCN 2024030554 (ebook) | ISBN 9781725352292 (library binding) | ISBN 9781725352285 (paperback) | ISBN 9781725352308 (ebook)
Subjects: LCSH: Archaeology–Vocational guidance–Juvenile literature. | Archaeologists–Juvenile literature. | Archaeology–Juvenile literature.
Classification: LCC CC107 .B36 2025 (print) | LCC CC107 (ebook) | DDC 930.1023–dc23/eng/20240702
LC record available at https://lccn.loc.gov/2024030553
LC ebook record available at https://lccn.loc.gov/2024030554

Designer: Leslie Taylor
Editor: Therese Shea

Portions of this work were originally authored by Mark Harasymiw and published as *Be an Archaeologist*. All new material in this edition is authored by Rosie Banks.

Photo credits: Cover (main) DeStefano/Shutterstock.com; series art (background) jijomathaidesigners/Shutterstock.com; p. 5 Gorodenkoff/Shutterstock.com; p. 7 (main) Inocybe at French Wikipedia/File:Rhinocéros grotte Chauvet.jpg_commons.wikimedia.org, (inset) Melnikov Dmitriy/Shutterstock.com; p. 8 urbancow/iStockphoto.com; p. 9 Western Arctic National Parklands/File:Backbreaking Work (8434276118).jpg_commons.wikimedia.org; p. 10 QINQIE99/Shutterstock.com; p. 11 Joao Pacheco/iStockphoto.com; p. 13 MarquesPhotography/istockphoto.com; p. 14 ShannonChocolate/Shutterstock.com; p. 15 Lysenko Andrii/Shutterstock.com; p. 16 Lysenko Andrii/Shutterstock.com; p. 17 selimaksan/iStockphoto.com; p. 18 George Trumpeter/Shutterstock.com; p. 19 General Cucombre/File:Pompei 5058.jpg_commons.wikimedia.org; p. 21 (main) RPBaiao/Shutterstock.com, (inset) Hans Hillewaert/File:Rosetta Stone.JPG_commons_wikimedia.org; p. 23 (main) Jaroslav Moravcik/Shutterstock.com, (inset) Chicago Daily News, Inc., photographer/File:Howard carter.jpg_commons.wikimedia.org; p. 24 US Government/File:Monitor model2.jpg_commons.wikimedia.org; p. 25 Monitor National Marine Sanctuary, Joe Hoyt/NOAA/Flickr.com; p. 27 (main) Kris1973/File:Trumna ze szczątkami Króla Ryszarda III.jpg_commons.wikimedia.org, (inset) Barthel ii/File:Richard III earliest surviving portrait.jpg_commons.wikimedia.org; p. 29 Bratislav Stefanovic/iStockphoto.com.

Some of the images in this book illustrate individuals who are models. The depictions do not imply actual situations or events.

Printed in the United States of America

CPSIA compliance information: Batch #CWSA25. For Further Information contact Rosen Publishing at 1-800-237-9932.

CONTENTS

Words in the glossary appear in **bold** type the first time they are used in the text.

AN EXCITING CAREER

Have you ever watched a movie featuring an archaeologist? Often, this character makes an important discovery about the past. Their job is an exciting part of the movie. There's some truth to these made-up stories.

In real life, archaeologists are trying to make discoveries about human history. To do this, they study the objects that people of the past have left behind. What movies don't show is the great amount of research, or careful study, that archaeologists do before they go out into the world to make these discoveries. They also often work in teams. Digging up history takes time and effort.

Archaeologists don't only study what happened long ago. They may study the recent past, or history from just a few years ago.

Artifact or Feature?

Artifacts are objects that people who lived before us made, used, or changed. Coins, clothing, and stones sharpened into knives are examples. Nonportable artifacts, or those that can't be carried, are called features. Human-made structures such as buildings or roads are features. Artifacts give archaeologists clues about how people lived.

FINDING A FOCUS

Archaeology is about all of human history—that's a large field of study! One way to divide this field by time period is between prehistoric archaeology and historic archaeology. Prehistoric archaeology focuses, or centers, on people before they had a system of writing. Historic archaeology focuses on people who had written records. These time periods can be divided even more.

Archaeologists often focus on a **geographic** region too. For example, an archaeologist might study prehistoric Native peoples who lived in the New York area. Trying to become an **expert** on all Native Americans in all time periods across North America would be much too hard.

People who didn't have writing didn't leave behind records, but often left behind artifacts such as weapons, tools, and art. This cave painting in southeastern France might be more than 30,000 years old.

FUN FACT

PREHISTORIC ARCHAEOLOGISTS CALLED PALEOPATHOLOGISTS STUDY DISEASES, OR ILLNESSES, OF PREHISTORIC PEOPLE. TEETH CAN REVEAL DISEASE IN ANCIENT PEOPLE!

DIGGING IT UP

Excavation is the process of digging up artifacts. It's a major part of some archaeologists' work. Sand, dust, soil, and mud can build up on top of artifacts over hundreds or thousands of years. Sometimes entire locations become hidden from view because of natural events, such as floods and **volcanic eruptions**.

In some cities, it isn't natural events that cover **sites**, but the people living there! People knock down older houses to build new ones. Roads are laid over older paths. Sometimes, many different structures are built in the same place over hundreds of years. Archaeologists may look for artifacts under existing cities.

Here, an archaeologist uses a sieve at a site in the United Kingdom. Water flows through the sieve, washing dirt away from the artifacts.

These are just a few of the basic tools that an archaeologist needs. They might pack them in a toolbox.

What to Bring on a Dig

shovel
digs into the ground to remove larger amounts of dirt

trowel
a handheld shovel that moves smaller bits of dirt when closer to artifacts

bucket
moves dirt away from the digging area

brush
sweeps dirt gently off artifacts

pick
a pointed tool that helps pick ground-in dirt off artifacts

sieve
separates small artifacts from bits of dirt

forms or notebook
to record what is found and where it is found

bags
to place artifacts in for storage and transportation

Tools of the Trade

Sometimes workers use bulldozers or other digging machines at an archaeological site. But these can harm some artifacts. The most common tools of an archaeologist on a dig are shovels and brushes. Archaeologists also use sieves. These tools are handy to find tiny artifacts that can be missed when digging through lots of dirt and sand.

But how does an archaeologist know where to excavate? They might match ancient maps to modern maps to find out where to start. They may see odd shapes or unnatural structures in photographs taken from airplanes or by **satellites** and drones. These may suggest people long ago changed the land. Sometimes finding a dig site is just an accident. Farmers and construction workers may dig up artifacts as they work.

Archaeologists also use **technology**. Sonar sends out sound waves that can bounce back when they hit buried or underwater objects. Radar works in a similar way but uses radio waves to locate objects.

FUN FACT

IN 1974, CHINESE FARMERS FOUND BITS OF A CLAY FIGURE WHEN DIGGING. THIS LED TO THE DISCOVERY OF THE ANCIENT TOMB, OR BURIAL PLACE, OF THE FIRST CHINESE EMPEROR, QIN SHI HUANG, WHO LIVED ABOUT 259 BCE TO 210 BCE.

A drone is an aircraft without a crew. A drone can take pictures or video from far above Earth. Sometimes these reveal ruins that are hard for people on the ground to see.

GETTING STARTED

Archaeologists usually dig on land that belongs to someone else. So, they take certain steps before they start an excavation. First, they must receive permission, or consent, to dig on the land from the owner or the government. The next step is to make maps of the site and take many photographs before the digging starts. The excavation changes the look of the land, so it's important to record how it looked at the beginning.

Archaeologists often divide the dig site into a grid, or system of squares, to help them record where artifacts were found exactly. They try to dig only in areas where they think they'll find something.

Grids help archaeologists remember which objects were located near each other. That can help them figure out what the objects were used for and who used them.

Before the Dig Is Done

As the archaeologist completes the excavation, many notes, drawings, and photos are taken of the surrounding area. Even the soil where artifacts are found is saved to test for chemicals or other matter. Archaeologists sometimes leave areas untouched. They hope future scientists will have better technology or tools to study those areas.

HOW OLD?

Archaeologists take the artifacts they find to a lab. They clean the objects and study them closely, recording what they see.

Sometimes, scientists try to find an artifact's age. All living things contain **radioactive** atoms of carbon called carbon-14. Once the living things die, the carbon-14 starts breaking down at a constant rate. A scientist can learn the age of bone, shell, and wood objects by measuring how much carbon-14 in them has broken down. Carbon dating can identify the age of things up to 50,000 years old. Other kinds of radioactive atoms can be used to date objects made of rocks and **minerals**.

FUN FACT

STUDYING ATOMS OF THE ELEMENT CALLED ARGON IN OBJECTS CAN DATE OBJECTS BILLIONS OF YEARS OLD!

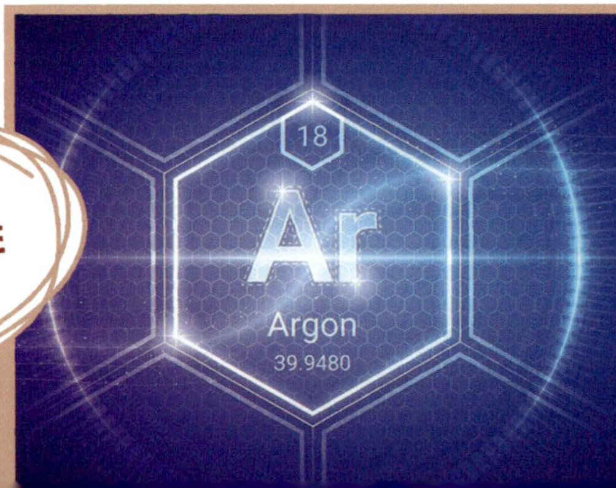

Sometimes dating an object is easy, such as a coin with a date on it. Objects found near the coin are often dated using the coin's age. That's called cross dating.

NOW WHAT?

Once archaeologists closely study the artifacts they've found, they write a report about their findings. They use the facts they've gathered and combine them with what other scientists have learned about the people and history of a place. Then, they explain what they think happened at the site and why they think their findings may be important.

Their **interpretation** is an educated guess, also called a hypothesis. It uses artifacts as clues. An interpretation is a lot like piecing together a story without knowing all the facts. The farther back in time, the harder it is to understand everything about a people or **culture**.

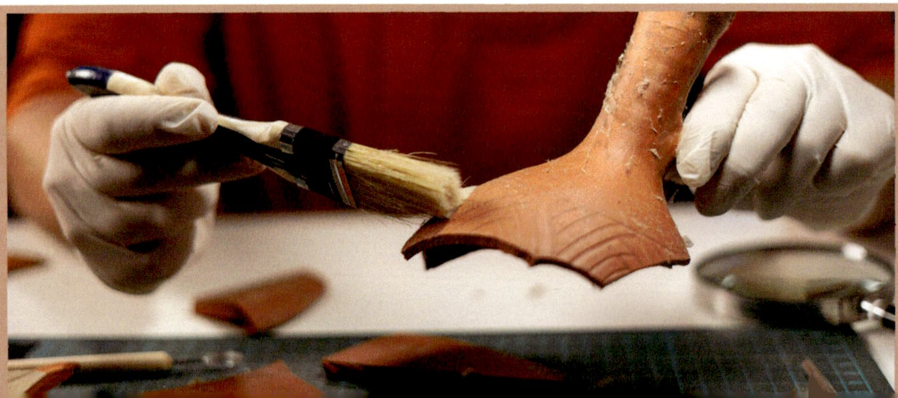

Archaeologists are a lot like detectives. They use the clues people have left behind to solve the mysteries of history.

Sharing the Wealth

Once an archaeologist decides on an interpretation, they publish the findings so they're available to other archaeologists and scientists. The information might explain some problem other archaeologists have been trying to solve in their own work. Publishing their findings also allows people who aren't scientists to learn about human history.

BURIED BY ASH

In 79 CE, a volcano in southern Italy, Mount Vesuvius, erupted. The Roman cities of Pompeii and Herculaneum were buried by many feet of ash and rock, and thousands of people died. No one could live near the volcano for many years. Over time, people forgot about the cities.

In 1709, a person digging a well unearthed a statue at Herculaneum. Pompeii was found under a vineyard in 1748. Archaeologists found items untouched since the eruption, such as ovens containing loaves of bread and jars holding fruit. They even uncovered skeletons of people who died. About one-third of Pompeii is still buried under ash.

jars found at Pompeii

The Temple of Apollo is just one of the many buildings excavated at Pompeii. It's shown here with Mount Vesuvius in the background.

Preserved

The ruins of Pompeii and Herculaneum are important because they provide a "snapshot" of ancient Roman cities. Other ancient cities, such as Rome, have had people living in them for thousands of years. Newer structures make it hard to have a good picture of what life was like long ago.

ACCIDENTAL ARCHAEOLOGY

In 1799, French soldiers digging in the ground in Rosetta, Egypt, found a stone with writing on it. They knew it was something important.

The stone had a date that meant March 27 and a year that meant 196 BCE. It featured three kinds of writing. One was ancient Greek, and the other two were the Egyptian demotic and hieroglyphic writing systems. No one living knew how to read either of the Egyptian scripts, or writings. When people figured out the three kinds of writing said the same message, they realized the Greek could be used to understand the Egyptian scripts. Many raced to be the first to **translate** the messages.

FUN FACT

THE ROSETTA STONE IS A PART OF A LARGER STONE. ARCHAEOLOGISTS HAVE TRIED TO FIND THE REST BUT HAVEN'T BEEN ABLE TO.

The Rosetta Stone continues to be an object of great interest today.

More Facts About the Rosetta Stone

- The stone is 3 feet 9 inches (114 cm) long and 2 feet 4.5 inches (71 cm) wide.
- The writing was about the kindness of Egyptian ruler Ptolemy V.
- Hieroglyphs were a kind of picture writing.
- Demotic was a faster kind of writing than hieroglyphs, something like today's cursive.
- The stone is kept at the British Museum in London, England.
- It has writing on it that says: "captured in Egypt by the British army 1801" and "presented by king George III."
- Many Egyptians want it returned to their country.
- The words "Rosetta Stone" now also mean something that unlocks a secret.

HOWARD CARTER, EGYPTOLOGIST

Howard Carter is perhaps the most famous archaeologist. In 1922, he made his biggest discovery in Egypt's Valley of the Kings: the tomb of Tutankhamun, also called King Tut. Unlike other Egyptian tombs, robbers hadn't stolen this tomb's riches.

Carter and his team found King Tut's **coffins**. Inside the innermost gold coffin was Tut's mummy. Many other artifacts were found, including a golden mask, couches, thrones, vases, and chests, all covered in gold. Because the tomb was unharmed, it gave us a better understanding of life—and death—at the time of Tut's rule (about 1333 BCE to 1324 BCE).

FUN FACT

CARTER AND HIS TEAM FOUND TUT'S TOMB UNDER MORE THAN 150,000 TONS (136 MT) OF ROCKS.

King Tut's funeral mask

Howard Carter was an Egyptologist. This is a kind of archaeologist who focuses on ancient Egypt.

A CIVIL WAR ARTIFACT

Some archaeological features come from more recent history. In 1862, the USS *Monitor*, a U.S. Army ship in the American Civil War (1861–1865), began flooding during a storm. It began to take in too much water and finally sank off the coast of Cape Hatteras, North Carolina.

In 1973, a team of scientists, including an underwater archaeologist, believed they finally knew the location of the lost *Monitor*. They found it by tracing the path of another ship that had been towing it, the USS *Rhode Island*. They also used sonar and a special underwater camera to make sure they had the right ship.

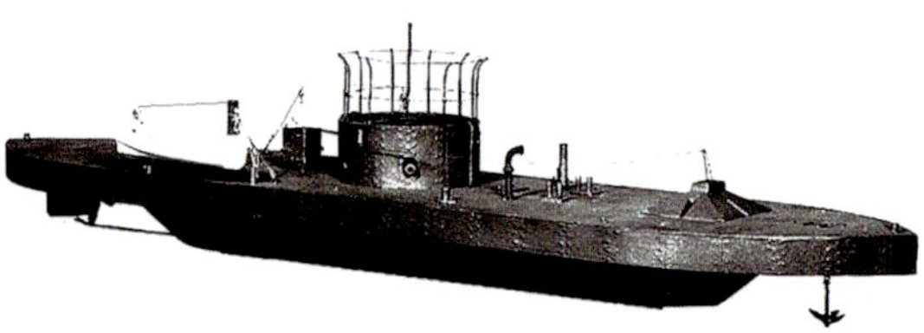

FUN FACT

DURING THE SEARCH FOR THE *MONITOR*, THE SCIENTISTS LOCATED THE WRECKS OF 22 OTHER SHIPS!

While some artifacts were recovered from the *Monitor*, the rest of the wreck became a national marine sanctuary. That means the ship and the water around it are protected by the U.S. government.

THE KING UNDER THE PARKING LOT

One of the greatest mysteries in British history was the location of King Richard III's grave. Richard, who lived from 1452 to 1485, was killed in a battle against Henry Tudor (later, King Henry VII). He was buried in a church in Leicester, England, which was knocked down about 50 years later. An often-told story said Richard's remains had been dug up and thrown into a river. However, a historian's research led her to a parking lot in Leicester.

In 2012, archaeologists from the University of Leicester dug in the area and found Richard's bones. After careful study, the remains were discovered to be the long-lost king's.

FUN FACT

RICHARD III IS OFTEN THOUGHT OF AS AN EVIL KING BECAUSE OF WILLIAM SHAKESPEARE'S PLAY *RICHARD III*. HOWEVER, SOME THINK THIS IDEA OF RICHARD IS INCORRECT.

King Richard III

Richard III's remains hadn't been placed in a coffin but in a grave too small for his body. He was buried again, with honors, at Leicester Cathedral in 2015.

DIG IN TO DISCOVER

If you want to be an archaeologist, become skilled at writing and research in school. These are a big part of archaeology. History, science, and math are important classes too.

In college, archaeology students often study anthropology, which is the study of humans and their cultures. They also take part in a field school. These classes offer experiences with excavations and lab research. Further study and a master's degree in archaeology might be needed for certain jobs too.

There's plenty more to find out about human history! Do you want to be the archaeologist who makes the next big discovery?

If you're interested in an archaeology career, volunteering for digs or at museums is a great way to get real-world experience.

GLOSSARY

coffin: A container that holds a body for burial.

culture: The beliefs and ways of life of a group of people.

expert: Someone who knows a great deal about something.

geographic: Having to do with the study of Earth and its features.

interpretation: An explanation of the meaning of something.

mineral: Matter in the ground that forms rocks.

radioactive: Matter that gives off energy when the things it's made up of change.

satellite: An object that circles Earth to collect and send information or aid in communication.

site: A place where something happened.

technology: Using science, engineering, and other industries to invent useful tools or to solve problems. Also, a machine, piece of equipment, or method created by technology.

translate: To tell what words in one language mean in another.

volcanic eruption: The bursting forth of hot, liquid rock from within Earth.

volunteer: To work without pay.

FOR MORE INFORMATION

Books

Gieseke, Tyler. *King Tut*. Minneapolis, MN: Pop!, 2022.

Murray, Julie. *Pompeii*. Minneapolis, MN: Dash! Leveled Readers, 2022.

Smith, Nicole. *Dig Deep: Connecting Archaeology, Oceans and Us*. Victoria, BC, Canada: Orca Book Publishers, 2023.

Websites

ArchaeOlogy: Clues from the Past
www.amnh.org/explore/ology/archaeology
Learn about mummies, ancient cities, and more on this fun site.

National Geographic: Archaeology
education.nationalgeographic.org/resource/archaeology/
National Geographic has more to say about this field and offers beautiful photos of archaeological sites.

What Do Archaeologists Do?
www.sapiens.org/archaeology/what-do-archaeologists-do/
Find out much more about this cool career from the *Sapiens* anthropology magazine.

Publisher's note to educators and parents: Our editors have carefully reviewed these websites to ensure that they are suitable for students. Many websites change frequently, however, and we cannot guarantee that a site's future contents will continue to meet our high standards of quality and educational value. Be advised that students should be closely supervised whenever they access the internet.

INDEX